ISLAND

A Story of the Galápagos

T0018774

Lava Cactus*

Waved Albatross*

Galápagos
Storm Petrel

Large Ground
Finch*

Woodpecker
Finch*

Greater Flamingo

Barn Owl

Magnificent
Frigate Bird

Red Mangrove
Tree

Giant Prickly
Pear Cactus*

Marine Iguana

Blue-Footed
Booby

Lava Lizard*

Lava Gull*

Zig-Zag Spider

Candelabra
Cactus*

Galápagos
Land Snail*

Galápagos
Fur Seal*

Brown Pelican

Sally Lightfoot
Crab

Galápagos
Sea Lion*

Galápagos
Penguin*

Galápagos Giant
Tortoise (Saddleback Shell)*

Palo Santo Tree

Swallow-Tailed
Gull*

American
Oystercatcher

Galápagos Giant
Tortoise (Domed Shell)*

SPECIES OF
THE GALÁPAGOS

*Endemic Species

Galápagos
Land Iguana*

Galápagos
Carpenter Bee*

Galápagos
Hawk*

Yellow-Crowned
Night Heron

Galápagos
Tree Fern*

Galápagos
Mockingbird*

ISLAND

A Story of the Galápagos

JASON CHIN

ROARING BROOK PRESS

NEW YORK

For Michael

An imprint of Macmillan Publishing Group, LLC
120 Broadway, New York, NY 10271
mackids.com

ISLAND: A STORY OF THE GALÁPAGOS. Copyright © 2012 by Jason Chin.
All rights reserved. Printed in China by Toppan Leefung Printing Ltd., Dongguan City, Guangdong Province.

Square Fish and the Square Fish logo are trademarks of Macmillan and
are used by Roaring Brook Press under license from Macmillan.

Our books may be purchased in bulk for promotional, educational, or business use. Please contact your local
bookseller or the Macmillan Corporate and Premium Sales Department at (800) 221-7945 ext. 5442 or by email
at MacmillanSpecialMarkets@macmillan.com.

Library of Congress Cataloging-in-Publication Data

Chin, Jason, 1978–
    Island : a story of the Galápagos / Jason Chin. — 1st ed.
        p. cm.
    "A Neal Porter book."
    ISBN 978-1-250-79993-7 (paperback)   ISBN 978-1-4668-2387-7 (ebook)
    1. Natural history—Galápagos Islands—Juvenile literature. 2. Galápagos Islands—Juvenile literature. I. Title.
QH198.G3C44 2012
508.866'5—dc23
                                                                                2011033797

Originally published in the United States by Neal Porter Books/Roaring Brook Press
First Square Fish edition, 2021
Square Fish logo designed by Filomena Tuosto

10 9 8 7 6 5

AR: 5.8 / LEXILE: 900L

I. BIRTH
Six Million Years Ago

The sun is rising over a lonely group of islands more than six hundred miles away from the nearest continent. The air is still and the sea is calm, but beneath the water something is stirring.

A volcano has been growing under the ocean for millions of years. With this eruption it rises above the water for the first time, and a new island is born.

Each time the volcano erupts, lava spews forth. Eventually the lava cools, becoming hard black rock, and the island

grows . . .   and grows . . .   and grows.

Many years pass. Frequent eruptions make the island treacherous, and nothing lives on it until . . .

. . . a seed falls from a tree on one of the older islands. It floats for weeks and eventually arrives. In time, a mangrove tree takes root.

Later, a seabird discovers the island and stops for a rest. She decides to make it her home.

Marine iguanas swim from one of the older islands. Their long claws help them cling to the slippery rocks as they climb from the sea.

Their powerful tails propel them as they dive to eat green algae below the water's surface. Their blunt snouts help them to crop the algae close to the rocks it grows on.

Life has arrived on the island.

II. CHILDHOOD
Five Million Years Ago

After one million years the island has grown.
The eruptions are less frequent, and it's easier for
plants and animals to live here. The water around
it is full of fish, and seabirds gobble them up in
feeding frenzies just offshore.

Mangrove trees flourish in sheltered coves along the coast.

Their roots form a tangled maze in the shallow water and provide a home for sea turtles and young sharks and rays.

Land iguanas float to the island on logs and branches. Once on land, they climb up past the mangroves and settle on the island's slopes.

After two million years, the island has become the largest in the group. Because of its height much more rain falls on it, and it's home to more life than ever before.

Old lava flows still scar its slopes, but it has erupted for the last time. Now that it has finished erupting, it will begin to sink very, very slowly—less than one millimeter per year.

There are different climate zones at different elevations. Rain and fog frequently cover its upper slopes, and the ground is covered with plants.

Farther down, the terrain becomes dry and dusty. Land iguanas burrow in the soil.

On sections of the coast, the crashing waves have worn the rocky shore into sandy beaches where sea turtles and marine iguanas lay their eggs.

Meanwhile, in the waters to the west, new islands are born.

One day a seabird leaves and lands on one of the new islands.
She starts a new colony.

Eventually, more of the island's plants and animals colonize the
new islands, including marine iguanas, mangroves, and
land iguanas.

III. ADULTHOOD
Three Million Years Ago

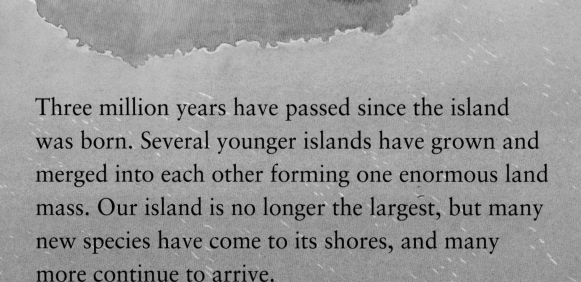

Three million years have passed since the island was born. Several younger islands have grown and merged into each other forming one enormous land mass. Our island is no longer the largest, but many new species have come to its shores, and many more continue to arrive.

Seagulls arrived years ago and now nest on its rocky cliffs.

Penguins have come from the south. The water surrounding the island is just cold enough for them to survive.

Frigate birds live near the coast. They are pirates and steal fish straight from the mouths of other seabirds.

Pelicans nest in mangrove trees and fish in the island's sheltered lagoons.

Over the next million years, more species arrive. Sea lions from the north establish colonies on the island's beaches.

In a distant land, a flood washes a group of tortoises out to sea. After floating for weeks, ocean currents carry them to shore.

Across the ocean, some cormorants are lost at sea. Luckily, they find the island and plenty of food just off its coast.

A group of finches is forced from its homeland. Here they find plenty of small seeds to eat.

The island is four million years old. It has continued to sink and as it becomes smaller, less rain falls on it. Droughts are more and more common.

During a drought, few plants survive. Fewer plants mean fewer seeds for the finches to eat. It doesn't take long for the finches to eat most of the seeds on the island.

Only large seeds remain because they're difficult to eat. Most finches' beaks are too small to open them, and they die of starvation.

A few finches have *slightly* larger beaks than the rest, and they can open the larger seeds. They survive, and in time they have chicks.

The chicks inherit their parents' beaks. Since only larger-beaked finches survived, only larger-beaked chicks are born. This generation of finches has *slightly* larger beaks than the last generation.

The droughts continue, and with each, the finches' beaks become a little larger. Over many generations, they gradually grow very large because larger beaks help them to survive the droughts.

Over millions of years many other species change, too. Some seagulls begin to hunt at night. In time their eyes become larger, allowing them to see better in the dark.

The tortoises' shells change shape. As the land becomes drier, their shells become smaller and turn up in front. This "saddleback" shape is better for keeping cool and navigating the desert.

One kind of seabird changes, but this is not due to the changing climate. The feet of these boobies gradually turn blue to help them attract mates.

Snails that live in the island's moist highlands are changing as their environment becomes drier. Their thick, round shells get smaller and thinner, and better suited for the new climate.

The cormorants' bodies get heavier and their legs become more powerful, allowing them to swim faster and deeper to catch more food.

On the island, they have no predators to escape, so they don't need to fly. Little by little their wings shrink, and eventually they are so small that the cormorants can't fly at all.

IV. OLD AGE
One Million Years Ago

After five million years the island has become
low and flat. I

Seabird colonies still swarm over its cliffs,

tortoises still plod across its soil,

and marine iguanas and sea lions still live on its rocky shores,

but some species can no longer live on the sinking island.

Thousands of years pass, the island sinks farther. Now it's only suitable for a few species—most of its plants and animals are gone.

Eventually, it is reduced to a small rock, barely rising above the water. It is lifeless once again.

Finally, nearly six million years after it was born,
the island sinks below the waves forever.

V. EPILOGUE
1835

It's been many years since the island disappeared.
There are fifteen large islands now, and on them
live the descendants of the plants and animals
that once called our island home.

The plants and animals here have adapted to the environment on these islands,

and many of them exist nowhere else on Earth.

Eventually, these islands will sink beneath the waves, too, and new ones will emerge.

As they change, their plants and animals will change with them, moving from one island to the next, somehow finding a way to survive.

These are the Galápagos Islands.

Charles Darwin and the Galápagos

The ship that appears at the end of this story is the *HMS Beagle*, and the man shown exploring the islands is the naturalist Charles Darwin. In 1835, Darwin spent five weeks observing the plants, animals, and geology of the Galápagos Islands. His observations caused him to think about where different species come from. In his day, most people believed that every species on Earth was created long ago and that they had not changed since their creation. What Darwin saw in the Galápagos eventually helped lead him to believe that species change, or evolve, over time. Twenty-four years after the voyage, he published *On the Origin of Species*, in which he explained how and why species evolve. His theory, called *evolution by natural selection*, was revolutionary. Instead of an unchanging world with fixed species, Darwin saw that living things are constantly changing. He saw that plants and animals adapt to their environments over time and he explained the process. Today, Darwin's theory is recognized as one of the greatest scientific ideas of all time.

Here's how natural selection works:

All animals pass their traits on to their children. Just like you might get the shape of your nose or hair color from your parents, an animal might get its beak size or tail color from its parents. Sometimes these traits help the animal survive, but other times they don't. If a trait is good for survival it will be passed on from parent to child. In this story, some finches survived droughts because they had a trait (larger beaks) that helped them open larger seeds. Because these finches survived, they were able to pass on their larger beaks to their chicks.

But what happens to traits that are bad for survival? They eventually disappear, because they aren't passed on. In the case of the finches, some birds had smaller beaks and could not open the larger seeds. They starved before they could have chicks and did not pass on their smaller beaks. In this way, traits that hinder survival disappear while traits that aid in survival remain, and over many generations, species evolve.

The Galápagos Islands

The Galápagos Islands consist of 15 large islands and more than 100 smaller islands and islets, located more than 600 miles off the coast of Ecuador. They are unlike any other place on Earth, and each island is different from the next. Some are large, green, and mountainous, while others are so low and dry they resemble the surface of Mars.

The islands sit on the earth's crust over a volcanic hot spot—a point where heated rock rises from deep within the earth. The rock melts when it nears the surface, and when the molten rock finally emerges volcanoes are formed. The volcanoes grow until their peaks emerge from the sea and become islands.

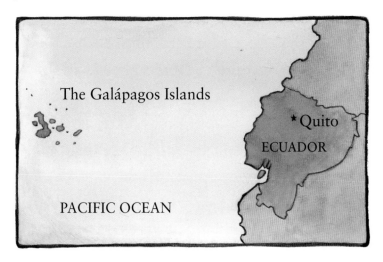

The earth's crust that the islands sit on is slowly moving over the hot spot like a conveyor belt. After an island forms, the crust carries it away from the hot spot. As it is taken away, the volcano stops erupting and the island slowly cools. As it cools, the whole island shrinks, and eventually the volcano sinks. Meanwhile, new islands form over the hot spot behind it, and the process starts again.

After an island sinks below the water's surface it is called a seamount. Several seamounts that were once islands have been discovered east of the Galápagos, although scientists believe that there are many more. The oldest is estimated to be at least nine million years old, but some geologists believe that islands may have been growing and dying on the Galápagos hot spot for ninety million years.

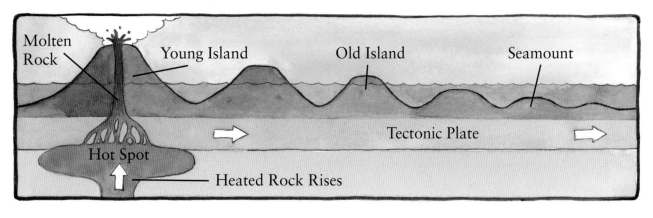

Endemic Species of the Galápagos

The Galápagos Islands have an extraordinary number of *endemic* species, or species that exist nowhere else in the world. There are more than 200 plants and more than 130 birds, reptiles, and mammals that are endemic to the Galápagos. Many of these species are endemic because they evolved into their present forms after arriving in the Galápagos. The marine iguana is one such species. This is how it most likely evolved: Millions of years ago, ancestors of the marine iguana lived in South America, and some of them traveled to the Galápagos. On the islands, some of these iguanas began to eat algae. Over time, they adapted to their underwater diet and evolved into marine iguanas. The iguanas that remained on the continent ate plants on land and evolved into the green iguana that is now commonly found in South America. Today, marine iguanas are endemic to the Galápagos because it's the only place where iguanas evolved to eat algae.

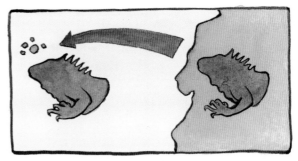

Iguana ancestors travel from South America to the Galápagos.

In the Galápagos, marine iguanas evolve, while in South America, green iguanas evolve.

Some species are endemic to specific islands in the Galápagos. Tortoises are one example. After the first tortoises arrived millions of years ago they spread from one island to the next. On different islands, the tortoises evolved in different ways, and today each island has its own type of tortoise with a unique shell shape. When one species evolves into many different species it's called *adaptive radiation*.

Author's Note

My intent in creating this book was to tell a story that would describe the geological and biological processes that led to the Galápagos Islands we know today. I based this book on the best scientific research available to me, but in order to create an engaging story, I have included events and details that are necessarily speculative. The majority of the story takes place so far in the past that there is no way to know with certainty how all of the events happened. The reader should understand that the processes of island formation, species colonization, and evolution described in this book are real and that my description of them is truthful, but that the specifics of the story are educated guesses and should not be taken as fact. This story is based on science, but brought to life through my imagination, and I hope that it will excite and inspire readers just as the remarkable islands of the Galápagos have excited and inspired me.

The following people assisted me with my research, and I am deeply indebted to them. Without their help, this book would not have been possible:

Dennis Geist, PhD.
Professor of Igneous Petrology and Volcanology
University of Idaho

Karen Harpp, PhD.
Associate Professor of Geology
Colgate University

Christine Parent, PhD.
Evolutionary Ecologist
The University of Texas at Austin

Heidi Snell, Galápagos Wildlife Naturalist
Museum of Southwestern Biology
University of New Mexico

THE GALÁPA

Darwin

Wolf

Pinta

Redonda Rock

Marchena

Isabela

Equator

Santiago

Fernandina

Bartolomé

Bainbridge Rocks

Rábida

Sombrero Chino

Seyn

Beagle
Rocks

Daphne
Islands

Bal

Eden

Pinzón

Santa Cruz

Puerto

Los Hermanos Islands

Puerto Villamil

Tortuga

Union Rock

Campeón

Enderby

Puerto Velasco Ibarra

Caldwell

Floreana

Watson

Gardner

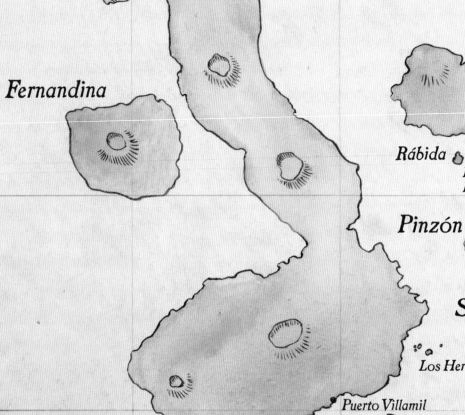

S ISLANDS

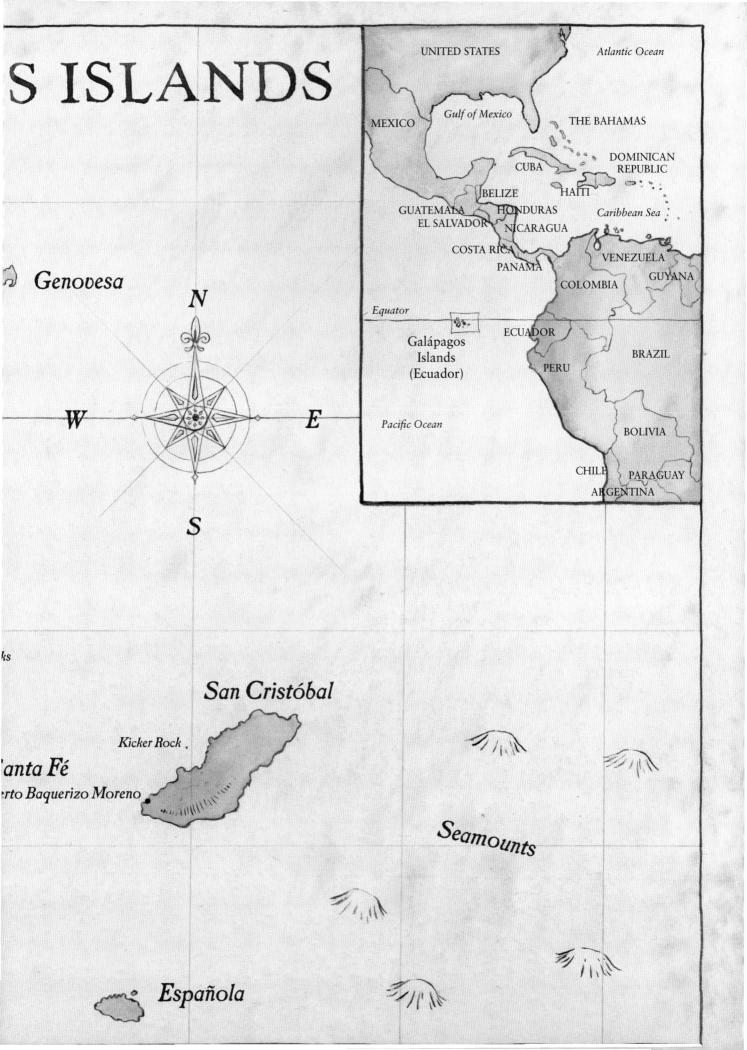

Genovesa

N
W   E
S

UNITED STATES

Atlantic Ocean

Gulf of Mexico

MEXICO

THE BAHAMAS

CUBA

DOMINICAN
REPUBLIC

BELIZE

HAITI

GUATEMALA   HONDURAS
EL SALVADOR

Caribbean Sea

NICARAGUA

COSTA RICA

VENEZUELA

PANAMA

GUYANA

COLOMBIA

Equator

ECUADOR

Galápagos
Islands
(Ecuador)

BRAZIL

PERU

Pacific Ocean

BOLIVIA

CHILE

PARAGUAY

ARGENTINA

ks

San Cristóbal

Kicker Rock

anta Fé

rto Baquerizo Moreno

Seamounts

Española